Whose Story
Is It
Anyway?

(Workbook)

This book is intended for 13 hour or week classes with emphasis on Impulse /Anger Management, Petty Larceny, and Drugs and Alcohol.

by
Bryan V. Veal, BA, CADC, CDVC

RoseDog✥Books
PITTSBURGH, PENNSYLVANIA 15238

RoseDog Books
585 Alpha Drive
Suite 103
Pittsburgh, PA 15238
Visit our website at *www.rosedogbookstore.com*

ISBN: 978-1-6376-4482-9
eISBN: 978-1-6376-4531-4

Table of Contents

About the Author

Bryan Veal is CEO of B and V Services, LLC. He was elected Student Body President at Abraham Lincoln High School and Selected to Who's Who amongst High School Juniors throughout the United States. He has a Bachelor of Arts degree From California State University, Sacramento. There he became a Brother of Phi Beta Sigma Fraternity, Inc. He pledged Lambda Kappa Chapter out of UC Davis. He has been a Licensed Counselor for Drugs and Alcohol since 1993 and a Certified Domestic Violence Counselor since 2002. Bryan was one of the first six students to complete the Drug and Alcohol Studies, a CAADE Certification Program at the College of San Mateo in California in 1993. He currently is working with individuals and groups in both capacities.

Foreword

The book was inspired by Bryan due to a lot of trials and tribulations in his life. An Autobiography will be coming soon. Bryan has done a lot of work on himself through Counseling. And Self-help groups. After embarking on a career of helping others he decided that if possible, he wanted to expand to reach and teach more people. Through his profession he has learned that it is not just the person who has had problems, whether it be legally or morally, but it is also the persons who lives are not what or where they want it to be. That they have not reach their potential or have stopped pursuing their dreams. A lot of times we become stagnant because of the stories that have been passed down generation to generation. In biblical terms that would be called generational curses. A person must go through some type of transformation in order to reprogram stories of our own and let them direct a path as opposed to having someone else's story in our head and letting it dictate our lives.

This book is meant to be an aid to redefining our lives and being open to the possibilities that we can pursue our dreams and desires and not be stopped. Entangled in this manuscript are spiritual principals that are guides for progress that will assist us in being in the emotional and spiritual realm to combat the naysayers, haters, doubters, and negative influences that create hurdles and stumbling blocks that keep us short of missing the marks that we desire. These are 12 concepts, derived from Acholic Anonymous, are principles that can be the bases or foundations of our spiritual and emotional transformations.

1. Honesty- we take sincere and a heartfelt look at our situation or situations. It is in being honest that we began to see that the stories that run our lives are not accurate, and it is then, that we can make an honest change.

2. Hope- We need help, because once we began to unpeel the onion, what we face can be overwhelming and as Jesse Jackson would say, we must "keep hope alive" and look forward to new possibilities in one's life.

3. Faith - This is the decision to step out on faith. It is only a matter of being willing to believe. Through the process that belief turns into faith. We carry this faith into the rest of the process by being willing to believe. We must begin to have faith it will work.

4. Courage - This step is really about courage to honestly look at ourselves. We will look at how our behavior has become warped, to justify our continued behavior. We are here to take an honest assessment of ourselves. Looking at causes and conditions of our behavior can be scary.

5. Integrity - If we have truly done a thorough job of introspection and evaluation of our assets and shortcomings, do we have the integrity to own up to it? It can be very difficult to be open and honest about our past behaviors. We begin to learn to do the right thing even though no one is watching.

6. Willingness - Now that we have accomplished an inventory of the good and not so good aspects of our character and behavior, are we willing to change them? All of them? Most people at this point turn to a God, or as in 12 steps, a higher power for spiritual empowerment.

7. Humility - Here we move further into action. We have seen where we have been selfish and self-centered. We practice being humble by realizing that we are not the center of the universe. We are all simply small parts of a huge whole. To be human is to make mistakes. Hopefully, our journey has led us to the point where we can readily admit mistakes and accept ourselves for being imperfect. We are asking for help and we are forgiving ourselves.

8. Brotherly Love – While we are preparing a list of those to whom we owe amends, it becomes time for the "golden rule". It is important to begin treating others as we wish to be treated. We must also learn not to judge others, but accept them for who they are, not our vision of who they should be.

9. Discipline - We are continuing to remove the barriers that can block forward sober growth. We are getting ready to sweep our side of the street clean. We are learning to become accountable while making amends to those people we have harmed. We are practicing new behaviors by facing our wrongs, so it is important to have this self- discipline. We are trying to try to correct our wrongs through action, not just words. We stay close to our sponsor during each amends to stay focused and disciplined.

10. Perseverance – We have entered the world of the Spirit and strive to grow in understanding and effectiveness. This takes practice and means we must keep on keeping on. We are beginning to trudge the road of Happy Destiny, and this takes diligence.

11. Spiritual Awareness – Here we continue to improve our conscious contact with God or our Higher Power, so we tap into that power through prayer and meditation. We become cognizant of the blessings we are receiving in our new life. We are learning to notice His handiwork in all aspects of our lives.

12. Service - Having experienced a psychic change that keeps us strong one day at a time, we are empowered to demonstrate the new principles by which we live. We remain in action in our daily life through example. We seek out and are available to help others in need. We continue to carry the message of hope and positive change. We strive to help wherever we can even in the smallest, simple tasks of life.

Dedication

This Book is dedicated to my Father, Albert Veal Jr. who exemplified all the self- worth attributes that are discussed in this book. A self-made man that instilled in me to be all that I can be and then some. His legacy will live on forever.

> "If you do one thing towards your goal every day, eventually you will get there!"
>
> **Albert Veal Jr.**

Week One
Breaking the Ice

1. Why do people steal?

    Write down 3 reasons why you believe that people steal or take things that do not belong to them.

    _____

    _____

    _____

    _____

    _____

    _____

2. What reasons and excuses do people use for acting out after getting angry or upset?

    Write down 3 excuses that you believe people use for acting out when they get getting angry or upset?

    _____

    _____

    _____

_____

_____

_____

_____

3. What reasons or excuses do people use for getting drunk, loaded, or intoxicated on a regular basis?

   Name 3 reason that you think people get drunk, intoxicated, or loaded on a regular basis.

_____

_____

_____

_____

_____

_____

_____

_____

_____

A. Why do people steal?

Possibly people steal for one reason and one reason only. We have made hundreds maybe even thousands of reasons or excuses. Here are some of the excuses I have heard in my over 20 years of counseling: If my baby needs something, I'll steal it if I have to., I was tired of my Mother buying stuff for my baby, so I stole to get something for my baby., There are not enough services out there., They are a big corporation they won't miss it., I needed it., I didn't have the money.

We can look at these examples by analyzing what is known by Dr. Rinowe as Thinking Errors.

The gentleman that said if his baby needed something, he would steal for it. Well, he stole from five stores in the same day and was caught at the fifth store. A member of the class asked him didn't you have enough after the first store and his answer was yes. It was then apparent that he was not stealing for his baby by the fifth store.

The young lady who was tired of her mother buying her baby things went to steal, got caught and had to spend thirty days in jail because she also had a warrant. She put her mother in a worse position, possibly having to take care of the baby full time while she was in jail.

A lot of clients stated that a lack of financial means was the cause of their stealing. They say that they cannot find a job. I put in applications everywhere and nobody called me.

Maybe its greed, maybe it is the rush, maybe its opportunist thinking that "I can get away with it". One thing is for sure these people did not consider the possible consequences of their behaviors and if they did, they ignored them. This would be considered thinking errors. In this country today we do not have a legitimate reason to steal. There are too many services as well as Churches and people who are willing to help. The problem is that people are not willing to ask for help or to work for what they want. In 2007 I myself had to avoid acting out on thinking errors. I had three back surgeries and the disability allotments were not enough to provide for my family, so I went to welfare and after having me sit there all day they told me to come back the next day only to deny me. I had a few choice words for the woman and supervisor in front of me. I stated that I have worked all my life and have never asked you guys for a quarter and you are telling me you can't help me because I made too much money in the recent past. But they did give me food vouchers and clothing vouchers instead. The entire experience was humbling from sitting in the welfare office to going to the food bank and Church food lines. There was a time in my young adult life where I may have resorted to activities that could have had negative consequences, that would have been far greater than standing in line at a food bank. Had I chosen to act on an error in my thinking, I could possibly be in a food line at the local county jail. It could be as simple as; **People might steal or take things that do not belong to them because they are not willing to do what it takes to obtain it in a legal fashion.**

B. What excuses and reasons do people use for acting out after getting angry?

Once again there was never a shortage of excuses or reasons. Some were: They made me do it. It was their fault. I was stressed out. My financial situation is bad. My spouse makes me act crazy because he or she keeps nagging me.

After listening to all the reasons or excuses one might ask one question. That question is why do children get upset or act out angrily? Almost 100% of the time someone will say right away, "because they don't get what they want". So, the next question is, why do adults get upset and act out? A silence usually comes over the room, because one would imagine that no adult wants to be compared to a child. The fact of the matter is that adults act out for the same reason as children, because we do not get our way. Think about it, no matter what it is, for example gas prices. Some of us can remember when gas was fifty cents a gallon, so when we go to the gas pump in my vehicles, we get frustrated and why, because we know now if it were our way, gas would be fifty cents again or less.

There is a three-step questioning process to dealing with an issue that has a person upset. The first step is to ask what is not going my way that has me upset. The second is to ask oneself what the options are to deal with this issue. Thirdly, ask which is the best option. In that process you will see 1. Why you are truly upset, 2. What are solutions to dealing with the issue? 3. How taking actions toward solutions can move you past the frustration, will be discussed more in depth in Week 10.

C. What excuse do people use for regularly being intoxicated, high, or loaded?

Of these three questions, it is this one, that brings about the most excuses. The most popular or favorite excuse is, to relax. Then there is, because they were bored. To party or to fit in. Because everyone else was doing it. To avoid dealing with problems. To escape reality. I deserve it after a hard day's work.

Let us first clarify the **relax** excuse because it is one thing to be relaxed and another to be high not want to do anything and then call it relaxed. Usually, a few chuckles follow that statement, because those who have experienced those times of being high and so lethargic that you do not want to do anything you just label that as relaxing when fact of the matter is you are high.

We could then ask these questions. Do you have an Uncle Charlie or an Auntie Betty that at every family function or get together they are inebriated or high by the end of the night? Or why are police always called to bars or clubs' late night? Why does the guy in the club or party continue to throw back drinks when they are already loaded? What is coming up for them? Uncle Charlie or Auntie Betty are fighting or crying, people in Bars or clubs are fighting, and who knows why the man or woman continues to throw back drinks. But one thing is for sure the people fighting, and crying are acting out on their emotions and the people tossing back drinks are trying to not feel their emotions. And here is the million-dollar paradox. We drink to not feel certain emotions, but alcohol and drugs in all actuality, magnify the feelings and emotions that we are running from. That is until we reach that point of oblivion where we don't feel anything, pass out, or black out. It is at this point that the consequences are usually negative.

People drink or get intoxicated on the regular basis to change the way they feel. This includes the famous or infamous marijuana, depending on what side of the fence you are on. People come up with all kinds of excuses for why they smoke marijuana. Those who do or those like me who use to smoke marijuana, (breakfast, lunch, and dinner), never once did it for any reason, than to get high or buzzed.

To bottom line, it:

The only reason a person gets loaded, intoxicated, or high on a regular basis is to change the way they feel. When clients try to tell me that they smoke it for any other reason than to get high one could ask them one thing. NEWS FLASH: Would you smoke it if it did not get you high? I have never had someone tell me yes, not even medicinal marijuana card carrying members have argued that point.

If a person were totally content with who they were and where they were at the time, they thought about getting high, there would be absolutely no reason to get high. Many eyebrows go up with that statement. One could have them look to see if their usage is based on a feeling of being uncomfortable in their own skin, in that moment. Like the guy who has not had a drink in a while and then says, "I need a drink". The same for that person who has not smoked weed in a few days or for a few hours then he says, "I need a joint or blunt". That thought is triggered by a feeling of discomfort when sober. For heroin addicts it can be triggered by a physical feeling of discomfort where the user convinces himself or herself that they need the drug to feel normal. But remember normal does not mean natural. The user's state might be normal because they do it so often, but they are far from natural because they are under the influence of a mood- and mind-altering chemical.

Questions: Whose Story Is It Anyway?
Chapter One

What is the universal reason that people steal or take things that do not belong to them?

_____
_____
_____
_____
_____
_____
_____
_____
_____

What is the universal reason that anyone gets angry and acts out?

_____
_____
_____
_____
_____
_____
_____
_____
_____

What reason have you learned to be the universal reason that people drink, get intoxicated or loaded on a regular basis?

_____

_____

_____

_____

_____

_____

_____

_____

_____

Week Two
Total Behavior

1. What do you think are the four elements of a person's behavior?

_____

_____

_____

_____

_____

_____

_____

_____

_____

A person's total behavior is made up of four basic elements: Thinking, Feelings, Acting, and physiology.

In **acting** we physically and outwardly display behavior towards someone or situation. This can be expressed physically or verbally.

In **thinking,** our thoughts sometimes run ramped and sometimes not much at all. Sometimes they are accurate and sometimes not so accurate. Sometimes they are healthy, and sometimes not so healthy. None the less we all have thoughts, and the key is what we do with those thoughts. A popular question is, can we control our thoughts? In the following chapters we will see that we might not be able to stop a thought from coming but we can sure have input on how we react or respond to that thought.

Our **feelings,** although sometimes hard to identify or label, do seem to dictate most of our actions, until we learn that our feelings are simply that, feelings, and do not have to dictate our behaviors. For example, we can feel sad without crying or feel happy without smiling. It could also be that we use our actions to cover up feelings.

Physiology, which is comprised of our bodies usually displays that something is going on with us. Such as being sick from stress, headaches, blood pressure problems, hives, shingles, skin discolorations. Doctors are is attributing a lot of illnesses and pains in the human body to our total behaviors.

We can elaborate and discuss how each aspect of total behavior is experienced in our lives. In the following chapters we are going to look at how we blame forces outside of ourselves for influencing and manipulating our decisions and choices. We will look at how we blame others or society for our choices, when the fact of the matter is, we do what we do, and either we ignore the consequences, or we don't think about the possible consequences, before we do what we do. A Professor once told me that in Greek philosophy they believed, if I do this, this might happen or if I do that, that might happen. Here in the United States most of us say, I am going to do this because I want this to happen, ignoring the other potential consequences.

What are the four elements of total behavior?

_____
_____
_____
_____
_____
_____
_____
_____

In what ways have you realized that your total behaviors have been displayed or have affected your life positively or negatively.

_____

_____

_____

_____

_____

_____

_____

_____

_____

_____

WEEK 3
Physical Needs in Life
Emotional Needs in Life

1. What are our physical needs in Life?

Can you name 3 physical needs of a human beings in life and why we need them?

_____

_____

_____

_____

_____

_____

_____

_____

a. Water- because our bodies are comprised of 70-80% fluid.
b. Food- for our nutritional value.
c. Shelter- to protect us from the elements which can kill you.

2. What are our 5 emotional needs in life? Also known as driving and basic needs.

What do think our 5 emotional needs or basic and driving needs in life as human beings?

_____

_____

_____

_____

_____

_____

_____

_____

WEEK FOUR
Basic Needs and Driving Emotions

The Five Basic Needs in life are:
1. Love and Belonging
2. Freedom
3. Fun and Happiness
4. Power and Control
5. Survival

Most people have never looked at their emotional needs. But everyone is driven by at least one of them at one time or another. If a person were asked what they are, usually they say **love** first, but the rest of them are not easy to see. There are questions we can ask such as: What do people in prison want? **Freedom.** What do children long for? **Fun and Happiness.** What drives casino owners and most politicians? **Power and Control.** The last one is **Survival,** but then most people ask, how is survival emotional? We will discuss each need separately.

If a person has an Impulse Control issue, we can easily see how these emotions are affected in every conflict. In a relationship with a significant other or a relative it is apparent that one might not be feeling the **love** or a sense of **belonging.** Primarily if one or the other is mentioning leaving or using words of hate or dislike and not wanting to be with that person anymore. If the incident gets too far out of hand and the police are called, then automatically a person's **freedom** is threatened. However even if the police are not called if the other person tells you what you can or cannot do or is trying to make you do something you do not want to do; they are threatening your emotional freedom. Fun and happiness are also natural emotions easily seen in children.

However, a person at any age, at one time or another, has an emotional need for fun and happiness. Once again when a person tries to control another person it threatens the fun and happiness emotion. In a relationship nine out of ten times if there is a conflict or dispute, it involves **power and control**. It becomes apparent when one party tries to control the others behavior or actions. Then we come to **survival** which is perhaps the most important but the least driving emotion of them all.

When Gang members are asked, what drove them to gangs? They say it is the since of family and belonging. One might ask what the driving emotions for a 25-year-old male with no wife, no children, just graduating from college signing a million-dollar contract, would be. Right away the men say fun and happiness. The same question is posed regarding women in the same position in the 2000" s and again they say fun and happiness. I will ask, what is the driving emotion for a casino owner or the Donald Trump's of the world? Initially people will say money and then we ask, what if it were not money what would it be, then they say power. Sheldon Adelson was once being interviewed on television and he said he wanted to be bigger than Steve Wynn (both casino owners). That mere statement tells us that it is about power and ego, not the money because both are worth billions and billions of dollars. A sensitive question would be, what is the driving emotion for a woman in an abusive relationship and she is being abused? The clients usually say survival or freedom but if were freedom or survival then she would have already left or called police enough times for him to go to prison. She perhaps might fight him back. She feels powerless, based on the statistic, that says it takes a woman 7-13 reported abuse incidents before she will leave the relationship (that is reported incidents, how many go unreported?), so it would not be power and control, actually that would be the opposite, a lack of power and control. In my twenty years of teaching domestic violence, I have never had a client say that the domestic violence encounter was filled with fun or happiness. So that leaves survival or love and belonging. Survival could be the driving emotion since some women are afraid to leave an abusive relationship for the fear that the consequences might be worse. Such as, brutal beatings or even murdered. So, the fact that over 60 women were reported killed in the state of Nevada between 2011 and 2013, could attest to women staying for survival purposes. However, so many women say "I stayed because I loved him or her" the most common driving emotion would be Love and Belonging. The woman is hoping and wanting so much for a loving relationship that she will hang in there where the other person is using their power and control to keep her there.

Let us look at Professional Golfer, Tiger Woods as an example. What his first was driving emotion coming out of College. Most say power and control because he wanted to win all the major tournaments and win all the money, as well as win more majors than Jack Nicklaus. He then starts bringing his dad on TV then his mother on TV then he gets married and starts bringing his wife on TV and then his children on TV. He gave us the impression his driving emotion was love and family. And then out of nowhere, the news comes out that he is almost beat to death by his wife, after she finds out about his infidelity and womanizing. One could say, he was driven by his desire for fun and happiness. This emotion was obviously running his life because he stops being discrete and became carefree or reckless with his behavior. To the point where it has ruined his life from where it was, and he has not won a major tournament since the incident. So, at this point even though he is living better than most, he is probably, by his standards in survival mode. He appears to be striving for power and control of his life and golf game.

So, which is the most important driving emotion of those five. We have many different answers. Maybe it depends on where you are in life which is the most important. One might ask themselves what is driving them in their life to do the things they do. Especially, if what they did, got them in trouble with the legal system or where they may feel stuck in their lives. If one looks hard enough, they will be able to see, that it is probably based on one or some of these emotional needs, driving them to stay stuck whether it be physically or emotionally. What they eventually see is that it depends on where you are in Life, that determines which driving emotion is more important at that time. In the next chapter I will discuss H.A.L.T. I will then show in week 6 how our emotional needs and H.A.LT., work hand in hand either in good ways or bad ways.

2. Which emotional need do you believe is the most important in your life and why?

_____
_____
_____
_____
_____
_____
_____
_____
_____

3. What would it depend on, to determine which driving emotion would be more important in your life? What circumstances might influence which driving emotions would be most significant in your life?

_____
_____
_____
_____
_____
_____
_____
_____
_____

WEEK 5
H.A.L.T.

1. H.A.L.T. is an acronym for what four words?

a. _____

b. _____

c. _____

d. _____

They are four things that we should not get too much of and never more than one at a time.

1. **Hungry**
2. **Angry**
3. **Lonely**
4. **Tired**

Hungry. Hunger is something that we pay attention to but sometimes we wait until we have symptoms from being too hungry. So many people admit that they had not eaten for some time prior to the incident. Many of the incidents occurred early morning, late at night and many before dinner or their evening meals. Clients have even admitted that they were hungry. When a person is hungry, they may not be able to concentrate. They may even get a hunger headache which makes it hard to focus. If you were to ask how many people read the labels on their food before they purchase it, less than more hands would go up. What do you think would happen to fast food restaurants if people really cared about what they ate? Most agree they would go out of business. How many people take time to eat a balanced diet? Most people say, "who has time for that".

Angry. What can happen when a person gets too angry? They can act out physically or verbally. It can cause high blood pressure, which in turn can cause strokes or heart attacks. They were angry about whatever the issue was and sometimes they were angry about another circumstance and attached it to the incident at hand. Some may have even had several issues that they were upset about. The problem is that most people have not learned to resolve their issues; they do the old "just let it go". You know the old oh I'm cool with it, but you're not really cool with it. Like that person who has an argument with their significant other then goes to the store and curses out the cashier for no good reason. Is it because they are mad at the cashier? Or is it because they are still mad about the incident that happened a few minutes ago with the significant other? Have you ever been hungry and angry, and somebody wanted to talk?

Lonely. Do people generally try to improve every relationship they are in, not just boyfriend and girlfriend but every relationship like neighbors or co-workers? Some people go to the same convenience stores every day and do not speak to the clerk. You may not take them to dinner but why not speak. Back in the day you could go to any house on the block and be invited in. nowadays you don't even know your neighbors name let alone be able to go in their house. What can be the outcome for someone who is lonely? Can loneliness have you hang out with people you would not normally hang out with? Can loneliness have you stay in relationships longer than one may want to because you do not want to be by yourself? Loneliness is a factor in a lot of confrontations of domestic violence. We hear women who are upset that their significant others are working too much which causes them to be lonely. It may also occur when either party is right or feel they are right about an issue and no one has taken their side, especially if the person winds up in a police car. That is a lonely feeling.

Tired. When a person becomes too tired, what can happen to that person? They can become less productive. They can have less focus and attentiveness to particular situations and or task. Lethargy and fatigue could set in. Tired can cover a wide range of areas also. A person can be tired from working many hours. A person can be tired of always arguing. It could be from not getting enough rest or sleep. A person could be tired of continuous negative results from bad or inappropriate decisions. In recovery it is known as being sick and tired of being sick and tired. When we ask someone how many times, or they try to tell us it is the first time, that something like this has happened, it alarms us. Because, that person, may be in denial about what is going on, in their relationships or their lives. We point out, that this may be the first time someone has gone to the hospital or to jail, but rarely is it the first time the couple has had a conflict.

My next question is, does anybody disagree that all four of these can affect our decision making? Usually everyone agrees. So, the mystery is, if we realize that they can affect our decision making, then, why don't we pay attention to them 24-7?

Remember the questions, ow many people read the ingredient labels on their food before they buy it? Who knows if they are addicted to sugar or not and how sugar affects the body? What would happen to fast food restaurants if people truly cared about what they ate? Who can say that they do the right thing with their anger, every time they get angry?

Who can say that they try to improve every relationship that they are in? How many of people go to the same AM/PM or 7-11 every day and never speak to or let alone have a conversation with the clerk. Some of us have neighbors that we do not even talk too or speak too. When I moved to Vegas, I would speak to people that I made eye contact with. Well, I was with a lady named Mag who said, "Why are you doing that? We do not do that here. And the longer I live in Vegas I found out that she was right, and a lot of people do not speak to you here. The next bit of advice I received was from a guy who said man I can tell you are not from here, DON'T LET VEAGS FLIP YOU. Up until this day I believe that was the best advice I have received in my 20 years here in

Vegas. This became apparent a couple of years later when I was working three jobs. One was graveyard at AMPM mini mart. This guy would come in every day at 2:00 am. We talked and were cordial. One day he came in and he said, "man you look tired." I said, "I am these three jobs are killing me." He in turn says" I will tell you what, I will get you one job making more on one than you have made on all three of your jobs". The very next week I was on the back of a garbage truck working for Silver State Sanitation Company. I believe I learned two valuable lessons from this experience, one is Vegas is about who you know not what you know, and the other is to not to let Vegas flip me. Had I taken on Mag's mentality of not speaking to people, I do not believe he would have offered me that job.

How many people think about eating right, exercising daily, getting 8 hours of sleep a day, taking vitamins regularly? After a show of hands, now how many people actually do it? Many may think about it, but few will do it.

Most people do not eat right. Most people do not deal with their anger issues in the best fashion. Most people do not try to improve all their relationships. And most people do not take care of their health.

In the next chapter we will see how our Emotional Needs are attached to H.A.L.T. and influence our choice and decision making.

Week Five

2. After reading chapter four, write one way that HALT had played a part in your behavior's or effected your emotional well-being. For example, what happens when you get too hungry, angry, lonely, or tired?

_____

_____

_____

_____

_____

_____

_____

_____

_____

WEEK 6
How Basic Needs and H.A.L.T. ,
Manifest and influence our decision Making.

In dealing with Domestic violence, anger management, and impulse control it is easy to see the correlation between our behavior and our feelings, which in turn, are driven by our emotions and not taking care of ourselves. If one looks hard enough, he or she will find an emotional attachment in most of our decisions, not only when there is confrontation, but even when things make us feel good or fulfilled.

Here is an example: If a person is asked to describe the incidents of their domestic violence or when they acted out because of their anger, the following questions can be asked. They can be asked were they feeling the love of their significant other. Undoubtably the answer is no. The second question is, were the police called and what did you feel when they showed up? More times than not they say, "I thought I was going to jail". Their emotional need for freedom was threatened. Thirdly, the question is, were you feeling fun and happiness at the time of the incident? The answer to that question would be no. The next question would be, were you feeling self-control or that you had self-power? This question often requires a more in-depth conversation as discussed in chapter 3. What a lot of clients do not understand, is the fact that a person tries to control or impose their will over someone, means a person must feel the lack of control in the first place, thus when the power and control emotion is threatened, then we strive to get it back unfortunately, some use inappropriate means and ways, such as by force. The other aspect of power and control is that people look outside of themselves for there power and control, when fact of the matter is power, and control comes from with-in. There is a saying that it takes a strong man to be gentle. Another is our most rational decisions are made when we are calm. Then one can ask how their survival emotion was threatened. It would be displayed if they were in a serious fight or if they were taken to jail and had the fear of loosing jobs or places where they lived. The fear of not being able to pay bills, of losing a job or becoming homeless, due to the incarceration would put someone in survival mode. The mere fact of being incarcerated can trigger the need to survive outside of the normal survival instincts of eating, drinking water and shelter. You then can then connect H.A.L.T. with those driving emotions.

5 Driving Emotions or Basic Emotional Needs

1. Love and Belonging
2. Freedom
3. Fun and Happiness
4. Power and Control
5. Survival

H. A. L. T.

H-ungry
A-ngry
L-onely
T-ired

If one thinks about it H.A.L.T. It is 4 things that we have control over. If one thinks about it most successful or people who seem to be most comfortable are those who eat right or take care of their health. They also seem to control their tempers and attitudes better than most. They do not seem to display anger as much as those who lives are in turmoil. They seem to strive on healthy relationships and do not appear to be lonely. They usually belong to a gym or exercise regularly, so they do not appear to be tired or lethargic.

Our basic needs on the other hand are often dealing with other people and life situations that affect our emotional well being. There are going to be times in life when we are not feeling the love or belonging from people closest to us or we are away from loved ones and become home sick (especially in places like Vegas, because most people here have moved from somewhere else or in the Military or a job that might require travel for long periods away from family and then there is incarceration which could explain the volatile environment).

Then there is freedom. The Question is do you have to be in jail or prison to not be free. A person can be locked up in their mind. Addicts and alcoholics are locked up in their minds. Serial killers are locked up in their minds. Feelings of desperation guilt or shame can be mentally and emotionally paralyzing. Being hostage to the past can prevent a person from being freed up.

Fun and Happiness is probably on everyone's radar. Everyone longs for some pleasure in life, Children long for fun and happiness. As a child summer vacation was a time when everyone went somewhere even if it were to Grandma's house just a few miles away. In some parts of Europe people's health plan include mandatory time off from work and vacation. There use to be a commercial that said, "sometimes we just need to get away".

Self control and Self power are important to one well being. Having self control and self power enables one to make sound and healthy decisions. If we take care of ourselves then those around us will be better off. After going through a divorce I realized that I must take care of myself in order to better take care of my children. Once I began fulfilling my own needs in a responsible way, I realized that the needs of my children were also being met. It almost seemed magical because most people think to put their children first. What one learns is that they deal with the emotional demands first, and that gives them more self control to not act on feelings and to make better choices.

If you are breathing, then you are surviving. The fact of the matter is that it only takes food, shelter and water to survive. However, our survival rating goes up when we take care of ourselves. We can do this by eating healthy, dealing with our emotions in a healthy way, improve our relationships and when we improve our physical health. When we take care of H.A.L.T., it makes it easier to deal with the times when people close are not showing us the love and belonging we want or times when we don't feel freed up or we feel stuck. Sometimes life just seems to lack fun and happiness. There will be times when we feel we have no control or power. And most of all sometimes we are in survival mode if we have a financial hardship, loose a job, or have a medical emergency. I am completing this book during the Covid 19 Pandemic, which began in March 2020, so everyone in the world has had to go into survival mode.

A good example of how H.A.L.T. and 5 basic or driving emotional needs can be positive is using my Grandmother Lurlean who at this time is 102 years old.

Grandma's house exemplifies love and belonging. When growing up all family gathering s happened at grandma's house. As a young adult into mischief and turmoil when I needed a break in the action I would retreat to grandma's house for the since of belonging and security. I believe to live to be 102 a person must be free from a whole lot of drama and negativity (stress free). She has a lot of fun. She drove until she was 82, she travels and has been an active member of her Church for over 50 years. She often says that she is blessed and happy to have lived to be the age that she is. I also believe you must have a strong since of self power and self control to have live 102 years. Her survival rating is very high because she has lived that long (not many can say that). She eats well. The only time I have seen her angry is at my three grandfathers that she has outlived. She is never lonely, people have to make appointments to take her places and her phone constantly rings. She is not tired yet at 102.

We will move from HALT to other ways to turn negatives to positives, to go from **I cannot, I am not, and I won't; To I can, I am, and I will.**

Week 6

In your own life give an example of how elements of HALT, and how Elements of Five Driving Emotions had been simultaneously active or pertinent in a particular situation or situations of your life.

_____

_____

_____

_____

_____

_____

_____

_____

_____

_____

_____

_____

_____

_____

_____

_____

_____

_____

_____

_____

_____

_____

WEEK 7
PAYOFF VS COST

Payoff is when a person looks at what benefit or reward, they are seeking from whatever they are doing. What is the benefit of being in a particular relationship, having a particular job, driving a particular car, or taking a vacation? Everything we do in life has a payoff for us or we would not be doing it. It could be the satisfaction one gets from helping others. It could be a momentary fulfilling of one of our 5 basic needs. It might be monetary gain that enables someone to have the fun and happiness or freedom they are seeking.

Cost is the consequences of what happens when a person goes after the payoff. For every choice in life that we make, there are consequences. Sometimes those consequences are good and sometimes they are bad. The Glasser theory determines that people simply choose to do what they do but they either ignore the consequences or do not think about the outcomes or consequences of their choices. The same thing applies to behavior. A person can choose to act a certain way and obtain certain benefits from that way of being.

The key is to determine if the payoff supersedes the cost. We can do this by weighing the scales of our choices. There is an easy graph to use, to determine if the payoff is greater or less than the cost.

Payoff	**Cost**

Once you list the entire payoff on one side and then the cost on the other, it will be clearly seen which side is greater than the other. The main factor to see is whether a person is in a healthy or unhealthy relationship. If more is on the payoff you most likely have a healthy relationship, if more are on the cost side, you will probably have an unhealthy relationship. If someone is in a class for being stopped for having marijuana in the car, the question for them is what the payoff of them is having weed in the car or smoking weed period. They usually say I was going to get high or sell it. Then they look at what it is costing them. It will be clear that that is the most expensive weed they have ever had, once they look at legal fees and any other cost like maybe missing work, etc. If someone is caught stealing, one tells them that that is probably the most expensive item that they ever had to pay for, that they did not get to keep. If they are there for impulse control, we want them to see that they may have one win the fight, but you must have lost the war because it is costing you money, now you have a violent crime on your record, and all the other consequences from the behavior. If a person simply ask, if I do this, this might happen or that may happen then they may decide to make a different choice or a more appropriate choice. Believe it or not some people still have a hard time excepting that they probably made a bad decision. So, they must look a little deeper.

They payoff vs. cost process can be used in almost every decision we make. We can use it if we are questioning ourselves about money spending habits, eating habits, or all of the should I or shouldn't I situations in our lives.

Explain how the payoff versus cost exercise has exemplified whether or not it would have been worth it for you to pursue or stay in a particular situation.

_____

_____

_____

_____

_____
_____
_____
_____
_____
_____
_____
_____
_____
_____
_____
_____
_____
_____

WEEK EIGHT
W.I.W.I. and I.I.W.I.

Fill in the Blanks

W _____   I _____

I _____   I _____

W _____   W _____

I _____   I _____

W.I.W.I. – I.I.W.I.

If you asked someone what W.I.W.I. stands for, rarely will someone get it right away. Was It Worth It.? Even as a counselor I cannot tell them that I think it was worth it because of what it has and will cost them as discussed. And finally, the question is if they could have done something to get the results they wanted without the negative consequences and after going through the payoff versus the cost and if it were worth it, they usually get that they could and should have done something different.

The process will not change what has happened. However using a different line of thinking that focuses on "What is my payoff vs. what will this cost me?" creates an opportunity to change past behavior and incorporate new skills of thinking and/or walk away.

I.I.W.I. would be if a person thought about, in the moment, Is It worth It to do what they are contemplating doing. Thus, if we ask ourselves what the payoff is versus the cost or is it worth it, we should, between the two thought processes, make a sound choice or decision. In turn this will give us a positive since of self-control.

WEEK NINE
Taking Control of Our Choices

In what ways do you feel you utilize your self-control?

_____

_____

_____

_____

_____

_____

_____

_____

_____

Realizing we have a choice and taking control of our choices are not always simultaneous. Sometimes there are factors that we must consider before making those choices. There may be times when we must have conflict resolution before making choices or we may first have to determine what we are really upset about prior to making choices.

Time-outs

Sometimes in the heat of the moment we need to cool off before we go off. So, let us look at adult time-outs. When clients here that, they say, "I'm not taking no time out, I put my kids on time out." An adult time-out is best described as one adult telling another that "I need to cool off for a while, but I am not ignoring you or being rude I just don't want to argue or fight. I will be back in about one hour and we can attempt to discuss the issue without arguing and fighting." In this process we can determine how important the issue is and start working on a solution.

Fair fight Resolutions

This process maybe as simple as asking someone when a good time for them might be to have a conversation. This conversation should be about I statements entailing what I want, what I don't want and what I would like to happen. A lot of people get here but they make the mistake of staying there. The second half of this process should be what the other person wants, does not want or what they think should happen. This conversation should happen on agreed upon time. The key is to not make the other person wrong with you statements but to set boundaries and to let the other person know what we are not ok with. A caring and understanding person will take your feelings and concerns into consideration if they are not attacked with statements like: you make me… …. or I hate when you………or Why do you…………… Most decision outcomes are better when both parties are in unison and agreement. Everyone wants to feel that their opinion is valid and respected.

Once a person has figured out what they are mad about and have reasoned or discussed the problem with whomever they have an issue with, then the taking of our choice becomes solution based as opposed to emotionally based, which usually come with negative consequences.

1. Give an example of how you could have used each of the Self-Control Techniques learned in chapter 9, in a past or recent situation.

_____

_____

_____

_____
_____
_____
_____
_____
_____
_____
_____
_____
_____
_____
_____
_____
_____
_____
_____
_____
_____
_____
_____
_____
_____

WEEK 10
The Three Step Process
to defuse anger and frustration

What is your process for calming yourself down when you are angry or frustrated?

_____

_____

_____

_____

_____

_____

_____

_____

_____

During the time out process or the fair fight resolutions waiting period there is a three-step process that one can take to deal with his or her anger or frustration.

1. The first step is to ask oneself; what am I really upset about? This may appear minor but many times we have misplaced anger. For example: We maybe upset about one thing and take it out somewhere else or on someone else. A better illustration may be that woman who argues with her husband then goes to the grocery store and takes it out on the store clerk if the clerk makes a simple mistake. Another may be the man who has an argument with his wife then goes to the bar and starts a fight.

Once we determine what we are truly upset about then we can go to step two.

2. Next we must look at the options we have to resolve our issues. Sometimes those options can be revealed by ourselves just by looking at what we are mad about and sometimes options appear when we take walks on our timeouts or through our fair fight. negotiation.

3. Once we have analyzed our options, we must choose the best one. Notice I did not say the right one because we do not always know what is right but most times, we can come close when we weight out the options. We do not always make the right choice, but we have better result usually when we examine our options as apposed to acting on impulse or feelings.

This has nothing to do with me.

Another way to resolve or not to get into conflict is to use self talk and tell oneself that whatever information that is being relayed to me has nothing to do with me. This may sound strange or peculiar, but two things will happen when you do this. One is that it will bring you present to the person or information being brought to you and it will have what is being said or presented not be taken personally. You see this the first time you try it. But it takes practice because a lot of times because if a person is very aggressive, it can put us on a defensive, so we do not take time to preface our thoughts with the statement this has nothing to do with me.

First, Second, Third, Fourth .... Thoughts

Our first thought a lot of times is impulsive and reactionary. I sometimes call it a Second National Anthem because so many people say it or do it. The term I gave it is "F It." Our **Second Thought** usually gives us that moment of clarity or that **30 Second** rule where we determine if the action, we are thinking about taking is better or worse, appropriate or inappropriate. You know those times when we say I better not do that, and we get that flash thought of a negative consequence. Or the times when we take that deep breath, count to ten or maybe we take that time out and walk around the block. Sometimes we need more than just a second thought we must talk to ourselves with a third, fourth, or fifth thought to do the least damaging thing. To simplify it is that thought that keeps us from getting ourselves in a jackpot.

Reactive or Responsive

Another concept to practice is to notice when you are being reactive or are you being responsive. **Reactionary** people act on impulses and feelings. They usually blame someone else for their feelings and that usually justifies their actions, at least in their minds.

A responsive person will determine that they are not ok with what has happened or what was said but they will use methods previously discussed to address the situation. This resolution is usually having minimal negative consequences, as a matter of fact a lot of times when we are responsive, we can see a positive outcome in a negative beginning.

Meditation may be the most healing of all techniques of dispelling anger and frustration. In meditating I have learned to encompass the previously discuss techniques sometimes from one to all-in-one setting. By the time I have just sat in a quiet peaceful place and considered all my feeling, beliefs, thoughts, and applied the processes needed to get relief that which I was distraught about, no longer has a strong hold on me. This sometimes does not take the pain away totally, but it always decreases the pain and moves us into solution as apposed to waddling in the problem. The problem if it is someone else, we can't change them and if it is something that has happened, we can't change that, we can only change our way of being with the issue.

Self Talking

Another way to resolve or not to get into conflict is to user self talk and tell oneself that whatever information that is being relayed to me has nothing to do with me. This may sound strange or peculiar, but two things will happen when you do this. One is that it will bring you present to the person you are engaging with and it will have what is being said not be taken personally. You see this the first time you try it. But it takes practice because a lot of times if a person is very aggressive and it puts us on a defensive, so we do not take time to preface our thoughts with the statement this has nothing to do with me.

Reel to Real

Some of my older readers may not know what a reel to reel is. For some of my younger readers it is what used to be used to make movies and records before CD's and DVD's were invented. The differentiation between the two is that Reel represents a story about what happened and Real represents what happened. Where do most people live, in the reel or the real? What industries in this country is more reel than real? The news, the reality TV shows, politics and tabloid magazines. When there is an altercation between two people and they are questioned about what happened, there are 3 sides to the situation. There is what 1 person thinks happened, what the other person thinks happened and actually what happened. That is what makes it hard for police because they are getting reel (story) from each person not what happened. We get this all the time in my Domestic violence classes when one is asked what happened in their case, they say the other person did this or the other person did that. For example, I remember a client saying, "I only knocked her hand of the light switch." He forgot to mention she just happened to fall over the couch into the coffee table and then hit her head on the end table. His story was that he only hit her hand off the light switch. Only the people there know what happened and the real would probably be a lot different than his story. I was introduced to Reel to Real by Maurice Burrell and helps one know when they are making something up or when they are looking at something for what it really is. In personal lives reel is usually the fantasy about what we wanted to happen, or what we expect to happen which is based on the story we created. An example used in CODA (Codependency Anonymous) is how we create a story about a person we are in relationship with based on how that person first showed up or how things were early in the relationship. Then they include in the story how they want them to be. REEL. The hardest thing to do is to get the client to stay focused on how things actually are. Real.

WEEK ELEVEN
5 Questions to Consider.

A. **Are you doing what you want to do?**_____

B. **Are you doing what you really want to do?**_____

C. **Are you working towards doing what you really want to do?**____

D. **Is what you doing working for you?**_____

E. **Are you willing to do what makes you happy?**_____

As we continue to move forward in solution for positive progress, there are five questions that we can consider. The first is, are we doing what we want to do in life? The second is, are we really doing what we want to do in life? Thirdly are we working towards doing what we really want to do? Fourthly, is what we are doing working to get us what we really want in life? And finally, probably the most significant of all is, are we willing to do what it takes to make us happy?

If you were to ask a room of 20 people if they were doing what they really wanted to do on the average of about 4 hands would go up. Most likely those four people have convinced themselves that they are doing what they want to do. They are probably doing what they feel they have to do, or need to do, to fulfill their survival emotions. This becomes apparent when you ask the second question of how many are doing what they really want to do. Almost inevitably the number of hands that go up initially is cut in half. Statistics show that 1% of the population in the world is doing what they really want to do. The next question is how many are working towards doing what they really want to do. Most hands go up with this question. For the few that don't raise their hands on either question, the rhetorical question is if you are not doing what you want or what you really want to do, or working towards doing what you really want to do, then, what the hell are you doing? And finally, the question, is that working for you? The paradox is that everyone is doing what they want to do, but how many of you are willing to do what it would take to make you happy. As we read below, you will see how we dissect each question.

Five Questions

A. **Are you doing what you want to do?**
B. **Are you doing what you really want to do?**
C. **Are you working towards doing what you really want to do?**
D. **Is what you doing working for you?**
E. **Are you willing to do what makes you happy?**

1 percent of the population is doing what they really want to do.

If that number is accurate then what is the other 99 % of the population doing?

A. Surviving

Maybe they are waking up, going to work, going home, and going to sleep.

In the United States what are most people doing in between going home and going to sleep?

A. Drugging and Drinking
B. Gambling
C. Sex Industry
D. Video Games
E. Social Media
   a. Twitter

b. Face Book
c. Instagram
d. etc.

There are in general 4 groups of people that make up the 1%. Who are those 4 groups?

A. The rich
B. Professional Athletes
C. Celebrities and Entertainers
D. The self-employed and Entrepreneurs.

Does that mean all rich people?

Some rich people blow their brains out.?
Some rich people commit crimes that ruin their lives. -B. Madeoff

Does that mean all Professional athletes?

Some pro Athletes are getting arrested for murders.
Some for illegal drug use.

Does that mean all Celebrities and Entertainers?

Some have drug addictions. -Whitney Houston
Some commit suicide or overdose.
Some have problems and circumstances that affect the other groups. – J. Beiber

Does it mean all self-employed and Entrepreneurs?

Most definitely not, but this is probably the group closest to doing what they really want to do. They are their own bosses and are doing a job or career for the most part strictly by choice.

What you want to do Versus what you really want to do.

Most people are doing what they want to do. However, most people are not doing what they really want to do because what they are doing it is not adding fulfillment, fun or happiness to their lives. As you read in Week 5 fun and happiness are desired emotional needs of all people. Most people will try to convince others that they are doing what they want to do because they are stuck in a rut or are in fear of change and or failure. They may feel that they cannot achieve what they really want to or that they are too old to pursue it. In my years of counseling, here are a few excuses I have heard for people not doing what they really want to do in life: I do not have the time., I am too old to go back to school., But what if I fail., I have been on my job too long to quit. Therefore, it appears that most people settle for where they are in life whether it is where they live, where they work, or even their relationship with a significant other. To the contrary most successful people invite or embrace the challenges, that keep most other people stuck. Have you ever noticed that most successful, rich and famous people have been married more than once, that most successful people relocate several times in their careers, that most of them admit to taking chances that they were not sure would work? Perhaps that's why pro athletes play beyond there productive years aside from the money because they have an insatiable desire to do what is fun and happy for them. I once had a successful businessman in my class that said he had to make a choice between his life of being a family man or accumulating wealth in the business world. For him he said he chose business, so he stopped getting married repeatedly, focused on his businesses and only had dating relationships. He became a successful entrepreneur in Arizona and California. He now owns Vacation property out of the country and is now married and enjoying his life after having done what he really wanted to do. Money is not always the end all either. You may have love skateboarding all your life, so you open a skateboard shop. You may not be making a whole lot of money, but you are your own boss and are doing something that gives you fun and happiness. Some people have convinced themselves to like what they are doing, and then you have those like Michael Jordan, Donald Trump, and Michael Jackson who have achieved the ultimate state of fun and happiness doing what they really wanted to do, which is known by Therapist Dennis Fitzpatrick as Ecstasy.

Are you working toward doing what you really want to do?

One would be amazed at how many people do not raise their hands when they are asked, are they working towards doing what they really want to do. If they are not doing what they want to do, or what they really want to do, and are not working towards it, then what are they doing? And that may be why it is believed that 1% of the country is doing what they really want to do and 99% are not.

Most of the country appears to be in the rut of going to work going home and going to sleep but in the United States most people are doing something in between going to going home and going to sleep. What is it? Perhaps it is feeding the addictions.

Drugs and Alcohol
Social Networking- Facebook, twitter, Instagram, etc.
Sex industry
Gambling

Do you think those 1% sit around stuck in addictions?

Is what you are doing working and moving you towards doing what you really want to do?

For most the answer would be yes but for some the answer is no. Some even believe the answer is yes but they never seem to get anywhere. Most of us know that relative or friend that always talks about what they are going to do but the conversation never quite matches what they are doing, and they never quite get there. Most people don't do simple things such as ask someone who has already done it or done any research. So most never reach the mark or settle for saying at least I tried.

Are you willing to do what makes you happy?

If you look at most 1%'s they don't only appear to be doing what they want because of the money, they also seem to be fulfilled with happiness and a peace of mind. The flip side of there success and happiness are that most of them had to put in years of hard work and sacrifice to get where they are. Whether it was education wise, going to school for years and years or training physically for years or maybe being self taught or self made through hard work and research, they finally reached a place of doing what they really want to do, This usually fulfills some of their happiness. And for some like myself in writing this book, most successful people speak about attacking their fears and pursuing their dreams.

So, when a person comes to the realization that what they are doing is not working, what must he or she then do? In the following chapter we will look at an avenue that will move one from merely existing to becoming a creator of what Dennis Fitzpatrick calls Ecstasy.

1. Describe what the quality pictures of your life would look like.

_____

_____

_____

_____

_____

_____

_____

_____

_____

_____

_____

_____

_____

_____

_____

_____

_____

2. Now answer the 5 questions from the beginning of the chapter.

_____
_____
_____
_____
_____
_____
_____
_____
_____
_____
_____
_____
_____
_____
_____
_____
_____
_____
_____
_____
_____
_____
_____
_____
_____
_____
_____
_____

1. After seeing that your Quality Pictures do not match your current life existence, how and what would be your process to achieving or obtaining your Quality Pictures.

_____

_____

_____

_____

_____

_____

_____

_____

_____

_____

_____

_____

_____

_____

_____

_____

_____

_____

_____

_____

_____

_____

_____

_____

_____

_____

_____

_____

_____

_____

WEEK 12
Creating Change

After finding out that you are not doing what you really want to do but you are willing to do what it takes to be doing what you really want to do and what makes you happy, then you are ready to create change.

Several questions at this point are pertinent about change, that a lot of people have never taken an in-depth look at. **The first is when does change take place?** It takes place some say when you want it to change. That answer can be negated with some dope users who want to stop using dope, but they do not stop. Some believe it takes place just by speaking something different into the universe. The response to that is perhaps, those people are just talking about change. Change takes place in the moment. For example, if a person say's they are not drinking anymore and they go out drinking every Friday night, the true test will not come until the next Friday when the routine usually starts. If he chooses not to go drinking, then change starts that moment. A lot of times we say we are not going to do something, and we may not do it for a while but sometimes we run on automatic pilot and we do what we are used to or what is normal because of our routines Sometimes this occurs even though we had every intention prior to doing it, not to do it. Like that person who says they are not smoking cigarettes anymore and a week later you see them with a pack of cigarettes, perhaps because they went gambling at the same casino and sat where they always sit, play slots and smoke cigarettes.

You then ask where Change takes place. Most people logically get that change must take place within. But most people say if he or she would just this or that then I would this or that. They also say when he or she does this then I will do that. Or if they loved me, they would……this is clear in relationships.

Take lady who says, "I will never be with a guy like that again." She has every intention of not being with a guy like that again in that moment but 6 months later you see her with a guy who appears just like the last guy or worse even the last guy all over again. This occurs because some where in that 6 months she either changed her mind or she convinced herself that this time things would be different. That is why change takes place every moment of every moment.

Taking Action

A person must set goals, then a plan to obtain those goals. Thirdly the plan must be implemented and carried out for a person to achieve the fulfillment of happiness.

A lot of times a person in a relationship will put their plans on hold to not upset the apple cart in the relationship, especially if the other person says they are not with that plan. The question then becomes can a person ever be truly happy if they don't fulfill a goal that they have and never even attempt to reach it. Some then say well a person should compromise for the relationship. At that point we see how people get compromised confused with sacrifice. If she wants Taco Bell and he wants McDonald's and he goes to Taco Bell, has he compromised or sacrificed? Most say right away that he has compromised what he wants to please her. I say perhaps he has sacrificed what he wanted to please her. Wouldn't the true compromise have been to go to both? I had a client who did that, and when they got to Taco Bell, she changed her mind. He became furious they began to argue, and he caught a domestic violence case, right there in the Taco Bell parking lot. Had he gone to McDonald's like he wanted to it would not have mattered if he she changed her mind or not. He could have been eating his quarter pounder while she figured it out. In Reference to the Man or Woman with the plan, the true compromise could be for the person to present his or her plan and then ask what yours is. And let us see if we can meet at the end of each others plan to achieve a common goal which is for each of us to be HAPPY.

In each moment, a person can choose to be a creator or a victim. Which one are you?

I had a professor who after raising 7 children and being married over twenty-five years, went to school and became a Lawyer and a Real estate broker.

My co-worker was the oldest student graduating when she obtained her master's degree at the age of 75.

Change is a constant in life. Looking at the areas in your life where you are not being fulfilled gives one an opportunity to pinpoint what changes are needed, thus creating a new way of being. There is one theory that we must conceptualize to ignite that change. It is the one thought that has kept many of us stuck or stagnant in one situation or another. The theory is this: In a bad situation there are two guarantees if nothing changes: 1. It will stay the same. 2. It will get worse.

2. After seeing that your Quality Pictures do not match your current life existence, how and what would be your process to achieving or obtaining your Quality Pictures.

_____
_____
_____
_____
_____
_____
_____
_____
_____
_____
_____
_____
_____

_____
_____
_____
_____
_____
_____
_____
_____
_____
_____
_____
_____
_____
_____
_____
_____
_____
_____
_____
_____
_____
_____
_____
_____
_____
_____
_____
_____
_____
_____
_____

WEEK 13
What Frequency Are You On?

What do you do when the radio in your car is not clearly on the station and you hear a bunch of static? Maybe you are in a happy mood and you turn on the television and the channel have something depressing on, what do you do?

_____
_____
_____
_____
_____
_____
_____
_____
_____

What do you do if you sense that a person is being negative or pessimistic? How about when a person has angry or confrontational attitude?

_____
_____
_____
_____
_____
_____
_____
_____

So what frequency are you on? In the last chapter we talked about creating change and doing what we really want to do. Well, we must also look at how we want to show up, and to be, who we say, we are. So, if you say you are a compassionate, loving, caring, honest, giving, peaceful, nurturing, kind, responsible person, then you must be committed to being that. Just as you would move the tuner until it is on the right station, putting it on the right frequency, thus removing the static. If we turn on the television and it is not something, we want to see, we simply turn the channel. Sometimes we must do the same things in our relationships and daily encounters with others.

If some one is bringing you energy that is not on the frequency that you are on, I say you have 3 choices to stay on your frequency.

1. Remove yourself from their presence.
2. Go down (usually) to their frequency.
3. Stay on your frequency and by attraction and modeling perhaps they will come up (rarely) to your frequency.
4. Stay committed to BEING who you say you are.

Sometimes life also has a way of interrupting our frequency. On February 3rd, 2020, My

Dad who had been sick off and on for a year or so, called me. He said, "Son I need you to come home now". The next day I was in San Francisco. I had been living in Las Vegas for over 20 years. I was facilitating for 3 Domestic Violence and or Drug and Alcohol programs. My 3 children and everything else I had accumulated were in Vegas. I was in the process of writing this book and workbook and a biography. I had to quit my bowling team I had bowled on for years. Needless to say, my life was turned upside down and the frequency I was on, was brought to a screeching halt, physically.

I say physically because mentally I never gave up. I had to figure out how to stay on my frequency in the mist of life circumstances and when my Dad passed away on May 30th, 2020 it became even more difficult. I was named executor along with my brother and responsibility was extraordinary because I was not only still responsible for affairs in Las Vegas but now San Francisco too. All this with the Covid-19 pandemic in affect.

I had to first secure a network of positive, encouraging, loving and honest people. Second, I had to reestablish what frequency I wanted to be on. And thirdly, stay committed to that frequency. Gradually I recommitted to my frequency.

In closing, I wish you much success and happiness in your life, because as old folks used to say, "Life is Short". Because people and life's circumstances can disrupt our frequencies, there are two ways to stay on your frequency or to regenerate your frequency. One way is to practice doing at least one thing towards your goal every day. This will remind you, of the frequency you want to be on, to achieve your goals. Another thing we must do, is stay committed. I believe for you to reach your goals, and to stay on the frequency you want to be on, you must stay: COMMITTED TO YOUR COMMITTMENT.

Acknowledgements:

Thanks to:

God, whom I am in co-creation with, almighty for giving me the courage and perseverance to follow through with this book from start to finish.

To Grandma Lurlean who provided a safe-haven for me and my cousins when we had nowhere else to go.

To Father, my brother and my sisters who never turned their backs on me and forgave me for causing turmoil and drama in their lives after Mom died.

To my children, Asya, Isaiah, and Roni for giving me unconditional love. And to their mother, Channon for birthing them and always being there.

To all my family near and far, past and present for loving me when I didn't love my self.

LRS who never gave up on me and through their believing in me, The Larson's and Vincent's who assisted me in developing and growing as a Man and Counselor.

Ahmondra Mc. For encouragement to move forward and to walk through my fears.

Thomas W., Manuel B., And Maurice B. for being the pioneers and founders of Healing the Father Wound, Mend on the Mend and the Love Supreme Workshops.

All the members and brothers from Healing the Father Wound, Men on the Mend and Love Supreme.

The men and women who attended the programs at which I worked and the counselors at the ones that I attended, because if it were not for you all I would not be who I am.

To Desi J. for being part of a memory that will be an everlasting thought to help me stay on the straight and narrow.

To my Phi Beta Sigma Fraternity, Inc. Brothers at UC DAVIS (Lambda Kappa Chapter).

To the Sigma Charter Members at Sacramento State. "Lone Star" "Frisco Slim" Oh yeah that is me. I was the first Phi Beta Sigma Fraternity Brother at Sac State 12-21-80.

To My Frat Brother John Kirtly who coach me into being financially responsible.

Thanks to Kat Williams who said, "if you don't have any haters in your life then you ain't doing shit in your life."

Thanks to my Auntie Evelyn who told me "Bryan no matter how many times you fall down, keep getting up and one of these times you will stay up."

To my friend and mentor Frank K. who allowed my friends and family to share in the peaceful, serene, and meditating experience of the Cabin.

To Bernice for her maternal nurturing and instincts, that has been part of my life changing for the better.

To Dennis Fitzpatrick for his mentorship and his encouragement.

To Unknown author: "Sometimes how we perceive ourselves is of lesser importance than how we are perceived by those around us. Maybe other opinions do matter."

To Jerold Serrell, E. Morgan, D. Smith, Irma, TNBA members Las Vegas, D. Haynes, J, Sanders, the McCoy's, Elverta, Kevin, PBA Rodney Garrick, PBA Hall of Famer Bill Coleman, and the rest of the bowlers I have bowled with and been friends with since the age of 12.

Special Thanks to Ronald Mardian who said, "Bryan you got to put this on paper."

If you feel slighted because I did not mention you personally, that was not my intention and just let me know. I will be sure to acknowledge you personally when my biography comes out. Let me know asap because it will be out soon!!!!!!!!!!!!

References

Dennis Fitzpatrick
Reality Therapy Certified (RTC), M.M.
Domestic Violence Supervisor 18 years, State of Nevada
Retired Supervisor for Board of Examiners for Alcohol, Drug and Gambling Counselor
online Domestic Violence, Anger Management, Alcohol-Drug Abuse and Parenting
Classes
2011-2020

LRS Systems Ltd.
 https://www.lrssystems.com
1900 E. Sahara Ave Suite 102 (Ground Floor) Las Vegas, NV 89104
2001-2020

Dr. Wayne Dyer 5/10/1940-8/29/2015
Choice Theory - Wayne Walter Dyer was an American self-help and spiritual author and
a motivational speaker.

Landmark Education-The Forum 1993 S.F. California

William Glasser, MD.
See Book Choice Theory
Harper Collins,1998

Men on The Mend- Thomas Warren And Manuel Baltimore-1993

Maurice Burrell
Founder of:
Healing the Father Wound
Love Supreme Workshop
Reel to Real-1994